Nan and Lisa Nan's Poems and Stuff

By

**Nan Tebrinke
and daughter
Lisa Nan Tebrinke**

© 2002 by Nan Tebrinke and daugter Lisa Nan Tebrinke.
All rights reserved.

No part of this book may be reproduced, stored in a retrieval system, or transmitted by any means, electronic, mechanical, photocopying, recording, or otherwise, without written permission from the author.

ISBN: 0-7596-8599-1

This book is printed on acid free paper.

1stBooks - rev. 3/15/02

Dedication

I would like to dedicate this poetry book to my family. That includes my husband, John, our son Aaron John and our daughter Lisa Nan. Lisa has poems in this book, also. Without their wonderful support, Lisa and I could not have written these poems. Lisa has, also, helped with the computer work. My family has always been there for me. May God keep them safe throughout the coming years. Who knows? Maybe we will finish this book this very year!

"A Positive Outlook"

This poem has won some awards and tells what I believe. Dr. Norman Vincent Peale has been a source of uplifting for me in his sermons and way of life.

"A Positive Outlook"
By: Nan Tebrinke

Being positive, it seems to me,
Affects how life shall often be-
One can worry, stress, and stew,
If, that is what one wants to do,
An attitude to look ahead
Eliminates both doom and dread.
To count the blessings life can bring
Would seem to be the better thing,
It surely keeps your outlook bright
From early morning 'til late at night.
Once you try it, then you'll know,
How truly it can help you so!

Nan Tebrinke and daughter Lisa Nan Tebrinke

The "Peace" poem is telling us that fighting leads to trouble, and one way or another.

"Peace"

We so need peace in this world of ours,
So many of us wonder why,
We can't find a neutral ground,
Of fighting or bombs in the sky,
Taking time to practice love,
And show it to others would be,
A wonderful alternative,
And it should begin with me!

Nan Tebrinke and daughter Lisa Nan Tebrinke

"Remembering Dad"

My dad was very much a spark of my life even up to his 95th year when he passed away.

He was extremely intelligent, and others have said this about him also. We are all so thankful we had him with us for many years.

Nan and Lisa Nan's Poems and Stuff

"Remembering Dad"

It seems like only yesterday
I would talk to you and say,
"Please push me on the swing today."
You would watch, as I would play.
In Algona (I was three),
A small park lights my memory-
Our favorite Friday time we had,
Just you and I, my loving dad.
We laughed; I swung or took to slide;
You caught me, always close beside;
Your many years were ninety-five
Travel, work, so full, alive!
You saw this twentieth century pass.
Eternally, fond memories last!

Nan Tebrinke and daughter Lisa Nan Tebrinke

"For Mother"

My mother lived until her 89th year. As I have said in this poem, she had an active talented life. As I said about my father, we were blessed to have her so many years.

Nan and Lisa Nan's Poems and Stuff

"For Mother"

When I look back at the years I grew up,
Many memories seem to come to mind.
Birthday cakes you made,
John's were checkerboards,
Chocolate were mine.
A birthday party on a cold January day,
I wondered where the Anderson twins had been,
They were at my house with others yelling
"Surprise!" when I walked in.
The 1939 Ford trips to California,
Each summer, we would go.
And all the clothes you made for me
With such talent, you would sew.
We said goodbye just four years ago,
And I hope you somehow know.
You always will be remembered,
We all love you so!

Nan Tebrinke and daughter Lisa Nan Tebrinke

"Thanksgiving"

We have always enjoyed a lot of blessings, through out the year. I feel this particular holiday is a time to give a big thank you to the good Lord Jesus Christ for so many good gifts!

Nan and Lisa Nan's Poems and Stuff

"Thanksgiving"

Thanksgiving is a wonderful day,
To reflect on the past year,
Wouldn't you say?
I can't count them all.
Some may be bigger
Some may be smaller
No matter 'bout that
They all are great.

Nan Tebrinke and daughter Lisa Nan Tebrinke

"To John"

    John and I have been hitched 28 years this year of 2001. He's always done so much for all of us; this is only a small poem for one with a kind and loving heart.

Nan and Lisa Nan's Poems and Stuff

"To John, November 18th 2000"

You've seen the year of 61'
And all the things that you have done.
You got to see the eastern states,
And slept in a Wal Mart parking lot relates
You give to us with love from the heart,
And are there when we need you
From end to start
May your birthday be remembered,
Because you are to us
From January to November,
A wonderful cuss!

Nan Tebrinke and daughter Lisa Nan Tebrinke

"Summer in Red Oak"

My girlfriends and I always went to the Red Oak swimming pool every summer as we grew up. As a matter of fact, I just about lived there! One memory I have is that sometimes I stayed in the water so long I turned blue! Oh well, I warmed up and went back the next day!

"Summer in Red Oak, Iowa"

Red Oak swimming pool in the summer,
Was the place my girlfriends and I would meet,
A certain area where we sunbathed,
Trying or was it not, to look very discreet?
When we first went there, so concerned,
Guys would see us,
Or was it our outerwear?

Nan Tebrinke and daughter Lisa Nan Tebrinke

"Murray"

Our dog was adopted from a dog pound in Clarinda, Iowa. He definitely became a member of our family. He was ours for several years. On May 1st, 2001 he passed on to another life in heaven. He will always be a pet to remember.

Nan and Lisa Nan's Poems and Stuff

"Murray"

Our pet is a doggy named Murray
He is a Schnauzer, who likes to walk in a hurry!
He takes he guarding as a serious jog,
And his barking can surely make your heart throb
But always he stays close by-
His master definitely knows why!
Because he is loved.
And loves his small home.
And never to the pound will he roam!

Nan Tebrinke and daughter Lisa Nan Tebrinke

"Christmas Reflections"

Christmas is a special time of year. We always look forward to it. So many times through the presents, tinsel, and decorations, we forget whose birthday it is. Each Christmas is special to our family.

"Christmas Reflections"

The Inn no room,
For our savior to be born,
That night so many years gone by
They would all so scorn
If they only knew what
The world had in store
The blessings of our wonderful Lord,
Why didn't they love Him more?

Nan Tebrinke and daughter Lisa Nan Tebrinke

"Being a Christian"

    I am a Christian first and foremost. This poem tells how I feel about being one.

"Being a Christian"

In this two thousand and first year,
It's hard to live when others have no fear.
We try to live as Jesus taught by His life,
Even if we sometimes have pain and strife,
He's always there-
He listens
He loves
He gently guides
And he promises always to be at our sides,
He only says to ask.

Nan Tebrinke and daughter Lisa Nan Tebrinke

"For Lisa"

My favorite daughter, my only daughter, is special person in my life.

"For Lisa at 14, August 24, 1995"

Off you go to high school today,
There are so many words
Your mom wants to say,
These next four years will go by so fast,
And, I think of many days gone past,
You are a young woman now,
And before we know
You'll be out on your own
And continue to grow
I thank God daily for you
And our son
Our wonderful gifts
Lisa and Aaron

Nan Tebrinke and daughter Lisa Nan Tebrinke

"Forgiven"

Forgiven is something I have thought about, often. It's wonderful to know you are forgiven.

"Forgiven"

Me-forgiven?
Even from times in the past?
When I didn't know you cared,
I choose to do "my own thing,"
Not knowing what my future would be.
You were always there
To guide, to love, to accept
Even if I didn't see.
Me-forgiven?
Only you could set me free!

Nan Tebrinke and daughter Lisa Nan Tebrinke

"Forgiveness"

Forgiveness along with forgive is also a wonderful blessing.

Nan and Lisa Nan's Poems and Stuff

"Forgiveness"

It's something to have in your heart,
If someone really believes,
Our Lord will give it in bountiful ways,
Forgiveness for you and me.
No need to fret,
Or to feel sad.
He truly does care about us all
But forgiveness comes
He won't let you fall.

Nan Tebrinke and daughter Lisa Nan Tebrinke

"Elva"

The poem Elva pretty much says the way I feel about her. She is a wonderful Christian lady. She has been there many times for me, and always a caring person.

Nan and Lisa Nan's Poems and Stuff

"Elva"

Elva was a friend of my mothers.
She has been there for me
And many, many others
So many times I've needed to talk
She listens when I call
Even if she's ready to go for a walk
I'm so glad to have her for a friend
It's like being with my mother again.

Nan Tebrinke and daughter Lisa Nan Tebrinke

"For Aaron"

Our son is Aaron John Tebrinke. I loved him right from the start! He is very talented and intelligent, as was his grandfather.

"For Aaron"

We have had you with us for twenty-two years
In the good times and bad times
We've smiled through the tears,
You are a senior in college
And we're proud of you
You've been a photo editor
A job just for you
We know you'll succeed
At anything you do
With God's special blessings
We will always love you!

Nan Tebrinke and daughter Lisa Nan Tebrinke

"Lisa"

Lisa is a wonderful daughter. I hope you enjoy her poems too.

"For Lisa, at 20"

For twenty whole years
You have been our girl
A daughter so wonderful
A distinctive pearl
No matter what you do
We hope you know
We love you so!

Nan Tebrinke and daughter Lisa Nan Tebrinke

"Our Home"

My husband John and I have lived in our home 28 years now. We are very fortunate.

Nan and Lisa Nan's Poems and Stuff

"Our Home"

405 Hammond is the address of our home
Nothing fancy or elaborate
But what we call our home
28 years we have lived here
a family of four
And many friends we love
Come to our door.

Nan Tebrinke and daughter Lisa Nan Tebrinke

"The Poetry Competition"

The poetry competition was for 650 plus poets. It was wonderful to attend and meet many poets. There were many subjects covered as we read our poems. Also, two Hollywood directors gave us helpful hints.

Nan and Lisa Nan's Poems and Stuff

"The Poetry Competition"

We left for Nevada
On the 9th day of September
So many events
I will always remember
I had such fun
Just meeting poets
We were friends right away
But I didn't know it
To hear others read,
As well as I
Made me feel a part
Of the balloons in the sky
They took our poems to heaven
With such a style and grace
Maybe someday
I'll visit that place.

Nan Tebrinke and daughter Lisa Nan Tebrinke

"Verna"

Verna is a wonderful friend and neighbor for four years now. We keep in touch, and she's become a great lady to know.

Nan and Lisa Nan's Poems and Stuff

"For Verna"

I am so glad you picked Red Oak to live
Your friendship has so much to give
Many times when I'm sad or have something to share
You have phoned or come by
And I know you care
You'll always have a special place in my heart
For you, my friend
Blessings do start!

Nan Tebrinke and daughter Lisa Nan Tebrinke

"Hospital Labor"

Being a medical and x-ray technician and a medical assistant gave me many good years as a job, and learning about people.

"Hospital Labor"

I attended and graduated as a medical technician assistant,
And x-ray tech from a school years ago
My first job was in a doctor's office where I learned my trades
Although
hospitals then were where I did a lot of tests
Using what I learned doing my best
But the labor in a hospital two times I recall
Giving birth two children
Was the best labor of all.

Nan Tebrinke and daughter Lisa Nan Tebrinke

"Days of the Week"

These poems for the days of the week are as I see them and how others do also.

"Sunday"

Sunday is a time for rest
Though many put it to the test
Relax, unwind, and let it go
But in the year 2001
It just ain't so
When I was young after attending Sunday school
Dad read us the funnies
Eating fried chicken or beef
But now at our house there is such a slight change
"Kentucky Fried Chicken" does the job just right.
Hey! I think I'll order some tonight!

Nan Tebrinke and daughter Lisa Nan Tebrinke

"Monday"

Monday has been called a "blue day" to some
The weekend is over
And workdays will come
To me it's a challenge to start a new week
And see what comes
As each day I seek
What I can do in 24 hours
Is part of the plan
And try my best to do
What I can
Though sometimes (if not all times)
It doesn't go as I thought
But maybe it's to do
Just what I ought!

Nan and Lisa Nan's Poems and Stuff

"Tuesday"

Tuesday is better than Monday
In just 24 hours after Monday it comes
In case this is news to you
Or maybe you already knew
You pick up where Monday left off
And get ready for Wednesday
But not letting your plan to be soft
Just think
Thursday comes right on time
And the weekend is just right to the rhyme.

Nan Tebrinke and daughter Lisa Nan Tebrinke

"Wednesday"

Wednesday comes and is day number four
You're over the hump day
If you are keeping score
The middle of the week
As some say with relief
It's that weekend stuff some want to see
Time off for workers
Is hard to beat.

Nan and Lisa Nan's Poems and Stuff

"Thursday"

Hey! Remember day 4?
Well, this is day 5!
Not many days before:
You guessed it!
Closer to the weekend!
Are you still keeping score?
We are over Wednesday
And a few more days in store.

Nan Tebrinke and daughter Lisa Nan Tebrinke

"Friday"

The last day of the week
We all look forward to
Time off for some
Others work through
There always are
Football games in September
Or cider autumn nights
Then comes December
Pizza seems to be a good Friday night treat
And the football guys don't get a break!

Nan and Lisa Nan's Poems and Stuff

"Saturday"

Saturday for our family
Is to be together
You see
We all have been
Away with school
And jobs each day
A day to refresh
That's what I say

Nan Tebrinke and daughter Lisa Nan Tebrinke

"September 11th"

On September 11th, 2001 we all have feelings about this event. Here are mine.

Nan and Lisa Nan's Poems and Stuff

"September 11th"

On this day of days
What happened in New York City
Is a day we always will recall
With sadness, and with pity
Who cased this to happen
To our wonderful land
This United States where we all live
We will always look back
And reflect
His comfort God will give.

Nan Tebrinke and daughter Lisa Nan Tebrinke

"Small Town Living"

Red Oak, Iowa is where we lived for many years.

Nan and Lisa Nan's Poems and Stuff

"Small Town Living"

Being brought up in this small town
And living here for years
From grade school to high school
In laughter and the tears
People have come and gone away
But some of us are still here
I have so many memories
And always hold them dear.

Nan Tebrinke and daughter Lisa Nan Tebrinke

"Garage Sale"

I love the season for garage sales! Keeps me out of trouble!

Nan and Lisa Nan's Poems and Stuff

"Garage Sale"

I must admit
There is a thing
I so enjoy each week
They are called garage sales
And I've found
Many bargains I do seek
I drive up the hill and
then down each Saturday
And stop when I see them
It's really amazing
These things are such beautiful gems!

Nan Tebrinke and daughter Lisa Nan Tebrinke

The Pacific Garden Missions asked for a few poems about their organization. I've never been there, but they have been a source I try to help.

Nan and Lisa Nan's Poems and Stuff

The old lighthouse it's called
Where warmth and fellowship glow
Many go there for a need
And find our Lord we know
How He can intercede
With a wonderful plan for all
A change from pain and strife
He'll be there when we call.

Nan Tebrinke and daughter Lisa Nan Tebrinke

"Holidays"

Holidays included are the ones through the year.

"Holidays"

What holidays mean to me
They are special times you see
With family members gathered
No matter how many or how few
With phone calls from those far away
Each one is special through and through
Christmas, Thanksgiving, July 4th, and Happy New Year
All of these times
Is something I look forward to.

Nan Tebrinke and daughter Lisa Nan Tebrinke

"60"

Being 50 is supposed to be mighty, but, I really think 60 is for me!!!

"Thoughts on being 60"

I have turned the
Even number gift "six 0"
I stop and think
What this occasion will show
How I have passed this "sort of" milestone
I really don't exactly know
I do look back and wonder
Where the time has gone
And what I have done
With each day
I do not know
I am so thankful
More than I can ever say

Nan Tebrinke and daughter Lisa Nan Tebrinke

"Yesterday and Today"

Thoughts of time are "Yesterday" and "Today" poems that I feel I can share.

Nan and Lisa Nan's Poems and Stuff

"Yesterday"

If we've lived our days
As we think we should
When the next day comes
Is it like we thought it would?
Twenty four hours we go about our own way
Sometimes wondering
What did I accomplish yesterday?
It is gone in such a short time
My, I am glad this does rhyme.

Nan Tebrinke and daughter Lisa Nan Tebrinke

"Today"

To live a life one day at a time
Is really the only way
To have the strength you really need
And lean on the Lord to say
"What to do?"
"Where to go."
And to look to Him
With trust
Is something I found
A peaceful way
For me a definite must.

Nan and Lisa Nan's Poems and Stuff

Nan Tebrinke and daughter Lisa Nan Tebrinke

"Thoughts on life"

These are what I think during the 60th year.

"Thoughts on life"

As I look back over the 60 years
I have been on this green earth
I ponder and wonder of so many things
From the present back to my birth
How, if, when, and where
Would I choose to live?
A live so full, so great each day
As an opportunity just to be here.

Nan Tebrinke and daughter Lisa Nan Tebrinke

"Time"

I feel time is very important.

Nan and Lisa Nan's Poems and Stuff

"Time"

Each of us have been give
The same amount of time
Twenty four hours each and every day
How we use it is a freedom
And use it wisely we should pray

Nan Tebrinke and daughter Lisa Nan Tebrinke

"Seasons"

The seasons in Iowa are what I reflect as Midwestern living.

"Spring"

After winter, spring appears
With the trees and flowers
And of course April showers
Slowly showing buds of green
Are warmer climates then winter brings
It's something I look forward to
No icy roads on which to drive
I am looking forward to summer too.

Nan Tebrinke and daughter Lisa Nan Tebrinke

"Summer"

Finally the warmer months have come
Swimming pools are open
Kids go there one by one
The air conditioners are turned on high
And "livin' is easy" as a old song implies
A picnic in a park
Or are they out of style?
Seems to me, we haven't been on one in awhile
I must admit I love these warmer months
Each one
And look forward to the summer's golden sun.

Nan and Lisa Nan's Poems and Stuff

"Autumn"

The change of season is awesome to me
Spring, fall, summer, and winter are something to see
The Midwest in autumn and the leaves golden glow
Are just preludes before the fall of snow.

Nan Tebrinke and daughter Lisa Nan Tebrinke

"Winter"

Winter can be my favorite time of year
The snowflakes are so beautiful
And Christmas time is near
Ice skating and sledding and building a snowman
Plus scooping snow off your car
Mumbling about that
Could surely be a sin.

Nan and Lisa Nan's Poems and Stuff

Nan Tebrinke and daughter Lisa Nan Tebrinke

"For my mom"

I think I wrote this poem as a gift for my mother.

Nan and Lisa Nan's Poems and Stuff

"For my mother"
By: Lisa Tebrinke

You were there when I learned to tie my shoes,
And to chase away all the blues
You helped me draw, color, and paint
And never to use words like "ain't"
Mother's have been here since the beginning of time
But there's no one as special as mine.

Nan Tebrinke and daughter Lisa Nan Tebrinke

"Mothers are good for something"

I wrote this for my mom because she is ALWAYS saying, "mothers are good for something." Yes, mothers are good for a lot of things.

"Mothers are good for something"

Mothers are good for something.
She would always say with a small laugh
But you don't have to know how to add or do math
To know how good mothers really are
They'll be there for you no matter if you are here or far
They are always in your corner, always on your side
And look at you with eyes full of love and pride
Even if you haven't been the best, they still care
(If you are wearing a clean pair of underwear)
Mothers are good for something, you see
Even if you don't agree, mine is still the best there can be.

Nan Tebrinke and daughter Lisa Nan Tebrinke

"My Friend"

I wrote this for a friend of mine.

"My Friend"

You've always been there for me
Whenever I needed a friend
You have given me a friendship
That will never end
You have always made me feel at home
And let me know I'll never be alone
I hope the sun shines for you
All of your life through

Nan Tebrinke and daughter Lisa Nan Tebrinke

"Grandma"

I wrote this special for my grandmother. I think it was for Mother's Day.

Nan and Lisa Nan's Poems and Stuff

"Grandma"

Grandma, what can I say?
About how much you make my day.
You always have a warm smile on your face,
Even if I'm a bit out of place
I know you'll always be there for me
And that fills me with glee!
Grandma, what can I say?
But I love you for the rest of my days.

Nan Tebrinke and daughter Lisa Nan Tebrinke

"Happy Birthday Dad"

This was a present for my dad.

Nan and Lisa Nan's Poems and Stuff

"Happy Birthday Dad"

Dad's been there when we've fallen from trees,
To bandage up our scapped knees,
Dad's there to help with the tricycle
So it will be easier to learn how to ride a bicycle
Dad's there to help us with school
And to make sure we know the Golden Rule
Dad's there when I need a talk from the heart
So then, I know I can get a fresh start
Dads have been there since the beginning of time
But no one is greater than mine.

Nan Tebrinke and daughter Lisa Nan Tebrinke

"To my friend (Laura Dahl)

I wrote this during a class with my friend Laura watching. I was bored, so I made this up a few weeks before graduation.

"To My Friend"

Laura was in Econ.
Waiting for the time to be gone.
Watching the president on TV,
Think this is boring and there is no more I want to see,
The marching band season is almost done,
When it is over, we'll be dance around and have fun!
The classes are almost through
Final tests to take
Not many things left to do
Soon we'll be walking down these halls for the last time,
You'll always be a part of the memories of mine,
Remember me when we are elsewhere
Even if we end up in Delaware
Maybe I'll see you in ten years
But, until then, will our eyes be filled with tears?
To say goodbye to Red Oak
Our hankies will surely be soaked.

Nan Tebrinke and daughter Lisa Nan Tebrinke

"My brother's bad dream"

My brother really had a nightmare about a giant Smurf when he was little. It has been a joke between us for years now.

"My brother's bad dream"

My brother had a nightmare one night
It gave him an awful fright!
It was about a giant Smurf,
My brother yelled, "Hey, get off my turf."
But the Smurf began to laugh and point,
My brother screamed and ran out of the joint
The Smurf ran faster and faster,
Yelling, "You can't hide, I am the master!"
My brother fell, and thought himself dead
When he woke with a start, and an ache in his head.

Nan Tebrinke and daughter Lisa Nan Tebrinke

"Snow Shaker"

I was twelve, I don't know what I was thinking to be real honest.

Nan and Lisa Nan's Poems and Stuff

"Snow Shaker"

Little snowman, in a snow filled world
Shake it and see if it falls
Smile through innocence
Now you are broken, even though you are gone
I still remain
But, I'm still here, not the same
So please smile in you snow filled world
Even though it has changed.

Nan Tebrinke and daughter Lisa Nan Tebrinke

"A game with a rabbit"

I wrote this because I was bored. Someone asked me to write a poem about a rabbit, and this is the result.

Nan and Lisa Nan's Poems and Stuff

"A game with a rabbit"

I once played checkers with a rabbit
Who happened to have a bad habit
He didn't play fair
And acted like he didn't care
He flopped his leg upon the floor
And just then there was a knock on the door,
It was my father who said
"Daughter, you forgot to make the bed."
And as he turned to walk away
He stopped and yelled, "hey!"
"How can you play checkers with a rabbit
Who has a bad habit?"
And I said, "Father, I can play with a rabbit with a bad habit
Just like one without a bad habit."

Nan Tebrinke and daughter Lisa Nan Tebrinke

"My Church"
By: Nan Tebrinke

I have been a member of the First United Methodist Church since the age of 5. It is a beautiful church.

Nan and Lisa Nan's Poems and Stuff

"My Church"

The First United Methodist Church in Red Oak
Is where we have been members for years
The beautiful stained glass windows
Are uplifting in happy times
And through the tears
It has a special place in my heart
And always will for me
The people who come there are very dear
And always will, you see.

About the Author

Lisa was born in 1981 and raised in Red Oak, Iowa graduating from Red Oak Community High School in 1998. She is now finishing her second year at Iowa Western Community College where she is a resident advisor and writes articles for her college newspaper. Lisa will attend the University of Nebraska in Omaha, Nebr. for the next two years with an emphasis in creative writing. Nan was born in Mason City, Iowa and lived there and Algona, Iowa a short time before moving to Red Oak, Iowa. She graduated from Red Oak High School in 1958 and attended Simpson, College majoring in music. She then attended Northwest Institute for Medical Laboratory Technique and graduated as an x-ray and laboratory technician in 1960. She worked in a doctor's office in St. Paul, Minn. Then moved back to Red Oak working at Montgomery County Memorial Hospital before moving to Iowa City, Iowa. There she worked at the University Hospital laboratories and later Mercy Hospital. She returned to college at Nettleton Business College, Omaha Nebraska in 1973 and graduated as a Medical Assistant.

She then worked at Montgomery County Memorial Hospital until 1973 until her marriage to John Tebrinke in 1973. After Aaron (their son) and Lisa (their daughter) births she was the Welcome Wagon Hostess in Montgomery County for ten years. She now does store demonstrations for five companies and works at the First United Methodist Church as nursery attendant. Nan's poems are based mostly about her life's experiences.

Printed in the United States
4555